A WALK WITH THE LIGHT IN THE SHADOWS

Paul Gaumer

Carpenter's Son Publishing

Published by Carpenter's Son Publishing, Franklin, Tennessee

Published in association with Shane Crabtree of
Christian Book Services, LLC
www.christianbookservices.com

Edited by Robert Irvin

Interior design by Suzanne Lawing

Cover design by Ashley Gaumer

Author photo by Ally Spangler Photography

Printed in the United States of America

978-1-952025-90-7

In loving memory of my Mom, Pearl Gaumer,
Pastor Michael Barr, Mallory Wierzba Jarvis,
and Roger Howerter.

AUTHORS NOTE: DISCLOSURE

My name is Paul Gaumer, and I live with Bipolar II Disorder. I am not a trained doctor, and in this book I share my own experiences with the disorder and my relationship with God. *If you are struggling with your mental health, please seek help from trained medical professionals who can accurately diagnose your condition.*

I do not have a pastoral degree. I am not an ordained minister, nor do I have any formal training in theology. Any interpretations of Scripture are solely mine. God has led me to write this book, and while the content may be from my personal experiences, it is He who gives me the strength to put it on paper. I truly believe He is speaking through me so I can share His compassion and love.

For the people who deal with mental health issues, this book may cause triggers as you read along. Be aware that I will be speaking of my mental health struggles, and some of those struggles are very detailed. *Please take caution as you read this, and if something does trigger an event for you, seek a trained medical professional immediately.*

If you or someone you know may be considering suicide, contact the National Suicide Prevention Lifeline at 1-800-273-8255 (en Español: 1-888-628-9454; deaf and hard of hearing: 1-800-799-4889) or the Crisis Text Line by texting HOME to 741741.

ACKNOWLEDGMENTS

This book would not be possible without the love and guidance of God. I am certainly not a seasoned author, but I sure do love to write. Every time I begin to write or type, I ask God to speak through me and use me as His vessel to bring awareness to Him. I want to ensure that the information I am sharing glorifies Him and allows me to spread my message of mental health awareness in the Christian community through Him.

To my friends and family, thank you. Thank you for always being there for me and loving me unconditionally.

To Kent: I love you like a brother. You are the most selfless person I have ever met. Thank you for being my friend at the times I didn't think I had any.

To Sean: you never gave up on me. You have been talking about the Lord to me since we were kids. Outside of the fact that I am a tremendously better fisherman than you, I concede that all of your "preaching" rubbed off on me. It just took a little bit.

To Connie: what an amazing woman you are. This was certainly not your burden to bear, but you took it head-on. You never judged me and always had an ear to listen or a hug to comfort me. I will never be able to thank you for that.

To Kristen: so many closed-door "sessions." Just your presence made me calm. You are strong and steady, and that was so soothing to me. Thank you doesn't seem enough.

To Cinda: thank you for graciously taking the time to review the manuscript.

To Jody: for being the best, most supportive boss I could ever ask for. Thank you for the discussions and suggestions as this became a reality. Thanks to Joe for letting me borrow all of the Bible commentaries, too.

To Gaspare: thank you for always checking on me and always having an ear to listen. Even in the tough days, I know you are just a short walk away if I need to talk. That means the world to me, and I can't thank you enough.

To my children and grandchildren, the joy in my life and God's gift to me of patience, love, and determination. At 23 years old, the last thing I thought I could accomplish was being a father. I was having a hard enough time trying to be a good husband. Then Shane, then Chase, then Ally. I couldn't ask for three more wonderful children. I have truly been blessed and love you all with every ounce of my being.

Of course, eventually they found their life partners, and I also consider them my children. To Ashley, to Chole, to Ryan: I love you as if you were my own.

Thank you for choosing to love my children. At the time of this writing, I have seven wonderful, amazing grandchildren. (Of course, I always hope for more.) Payton, Will, Theo, Hazel, Memphis, Denver, and Ellie: you certainly have Papa's heart on a totally different level of love. They say that your circle of true love isn't complete until your children have children, and that is so true.

To my children, my "in-law" children, and my grandchildren: thank you for forcing me to love deeply and with the patience only God could provide. I love you each so very much.

Finally, to my beautiful wife Jeanine. I have never met a more loving, determined, and caring person in this world. You took the time to understand my disorder and always seems to know the right thing to do or say and, all the while, you have dealt with your own health challenges. I want the reader to honestly think how difficult it is living 24/7 with someone who has a mental disorder. The uncertainty of emotions—sometimes minute to minute. Not only did she embrace it with unconditional love, she has never judged me. Jeanine helps me through the highs and lows, especially the lows, with patience, love, and understanding, while others would choose to run from it all. We have certainly had our challenges in our married life, but Jeanine has always handled things with grace and compassion. She has never left my side even though

I am sure there were times I made things unbearable and intolerable. Jeanine, you are my whole world, you completely fill my soul, and you are the rock that is placed next to God to provide stability in a sometimes unstable walk. I love you with all my heart, now and forever. Thank you for choosing to love me back.

CONTENTS

INTRODUCTION

In November 2012 I was diagnosed with Bipolar II Disorder. Leading to my diagnosis, I knew something was wrong. My mind raced constantly; I couldn't sleep. I would cry or get angry at the drop of a dime, my relationship with my family became more and more strained, and the most disturbing thing of all: I wanted to kill myself. It was all I could think about. My mind constantly showed me different ways to do it. I clearly remember coming home from work one night and approaching a center support of a bridge in the median of the road; I came dangerously close to driving into it at 85 miles per hour. At that point, it wasn't *if* I was going to do it. It was when.

In today's society, mental health and mental illness are used interchangeably. I believe that they are two very distinct situations that need to be addressed differently. I look at mental health as situational or environmental; something in your life has caused depression, anxiety, or hopelessness. Things such as not being able to pay your bills, the loss of someone close to you, a divorce, and so on. Many times, situational life events can be corrected over time with or without the help of medicine or professionals. Mental illness is chemical. There is an imbalance in your brain that causes deception regarding what is real and what isn't. Typically, this requires lifetime professional intervention and medication. This is not to discount the importance of addressing mental health issues. Situational challenges are very real and need to be taken extremely seriously. Only a trained medical professional can diagnose which mental space you are in, and you must find the best treatment for you. I just believe it is necessary to distinguish the two for context as you continue reading.

We all think of mental illness in different ways. People will label someone with a mental illness as "crazy." If I asked you to picture a "crazy person," what image would you see? It is typically someone with crazy eyes—cue picture of Charles Manson—with crazy hair, and they make no sense when they speak. The meme on the Internet of the guy whose hair is all disheveled is always associated with someone considered crazy. Albert Einstein, while brilliant, also was thought to potentially be schizophrenic, and he had his crazy hair. And of course, there's Dr. Frankenstein, who hadn't combed his hair in years! Well, folks, what

I have to say is so important: I combed my hair for you today.

I accepted Christ as my Lord and Savior in November 2000. I remember such fire and passion in my initial walk with God. Pastor Mike Barr gave a compelling sermon that day, and then he asked the congregation to bow their heads. He asked if there was anyone who didn't know Christ. He said now was the time to ask Him into your heart. I did, and I felt a sense of peace come over me that was unlike anything else I had felt. I became a child of God. What could be better? Asking for the forgiveness of my sins and the hope of eternal life through Jesus Christ. I was reborn.

A few years later my wife, Jeanine, told me I needed help. Of course, I told her things would be fine. I would get over it. It was just a phase. "I'm just tired." As the head of my household and father of two boys—we would soon add a daughter (more on that later)—how dare she question my manhood and ability to lead my family? She was out of her mind if she thought I needed help. It turns out, I was out of mine.

There was a day I went into my closet and looked at my shotgun. I went to reach for the shells, and they were gone. There were many nights of pacing the house just trying to get the demons in my head to stop. I found myself standing in the backyard a few times looking at the trees and wondering what it would take to get a noose upon a strong limb. How many ibuprofen would I have to take to kill myself?

I kept thinking of my family and the pain such an action would cause. I could see my wife screaming with tears running down her face when she found me. Those images caused me to hesitate. Forced me to take a step back and realize I didn't want to cause that type of pain to her or anyone else. It was early in the cycles of the bipolar, and the demons hadn't taken complete hold. I still had small remnants of rational thinking. I can only praise God for that now.

The one thing I didn't really think about was God. Oh, I prayed sometimes, but they weren't sincere prayers. Mostly they were asking God what was happening to me. Here I was, less than ten years from asking God into my heart, and I felt like God had abandoned me. In Mark 15:33, Jesus is hanging on the cross and He cries out in a loud voice, *"My God, My God, why have You forsaken me?"* That was the verse that kept coming to mind. *Why has God forsaken me?*

During the night, in one of my darkest times, I finally gave in. I completely focused my attention on God. I kept asking Him why He would take one of His children and give him such dreadful thoughts. Why would He cause such darkness and despair? And then I realized: the demons and their voices had stopped. My rational mind took hold for the first time in a very long time. God was listening! And He stopped all thoughts of self-harm and self-pity, even if it was just for a little while. At that moment, and from that day forward, I stopped questioning God and saw the light He was providing. He was showing the way to peace and comfort through Him.

The next day, I went to Jeanine and told her I needed help.

Once I received the help and medication I needed, I started to understand some of God's plans. I truly felt God had a purpose for me. Just a short time earlier, I hadn't known what it was. Now He has shown me the path—and this book is one result.

Throughout the book I will speak about demons. For people with a mental illness, this is a common description of the darkness that invades the mind. Being a Christian, my definition of demons is Satan, or Satan's soldiers who try to negatively influence a normal, rational thought pattern. Each instance of Satan's influence comes with the challenge of falling away from God and His love. This constant battle can define life or death. This is part of my everyday life and my struggle with keeping God at the forefront of my thoughts. You will see that I'm imperfect—but God already knew that. He is never far away and will fight the battle for me if I let Him. He will do the same for you. So far, I can keep the demons at bay only by His love, strength, and compassion.

I believe God wants me to be His voice in ending the stigma of mental illness in the Christian community. He wants me to share my journey of acceptance of Christ, to stop denouncing Him and questioning His plan for the darkness that surrounded me, and, finally, to see His light with the verses in His Word that speak to me. With my disorder, I still have bad days. That is just one part of the cycles of bipolar. But now, I immediately go to God and ask for His comfort and compassion to get me through the dark times.

God will not heal me. God will hear my cries and give me the strength to continue my journey with Him and be His voice for all to hear. God will not forsake you. God will be with you always if you follow the plan He has laid out for you. But you need to pray and then be still so He can reveal that plan to you. I give all the praise and glory to God for this book, and I hope it can be a comfort for you in the hard times as well.

In Christian love,
Paul

PART I

FAITH

Chapter 1

A WAY OUT

1 CORINTHIANS 10:13
"No temptation has overtaken you except what is common to mankind. And God is faithful; He will not let you be tempted beyond what you can bear. But, when you are tempted, He will also provide a way out so that you can endure it."

The purpose of the letter of First Corinthians was for Paul to identify problems in the church at Corinth. Paul's main goal was to teach the believers in Christ how to stay focused on Christ in an ever-changing, extremely sinful time. In 1 Corinthians 1:10, Paul wrote, *"I appeal to you, brother and sisters, in the name of our Lord Jesus Christ, that you agree with one another in what you say and that there be no divisions among you, but that you may be perfectly united in mind and thought.*" He left no room for interpretation. The people of Corinth needed to live in Christ so they could be taken away from a sinful culture and have eternal life in Heaven. This is not an easy thing to do when you struggle with the demons that often accompany Bipolar Disorder.

Whether real or imagined, God does seem to give you, at times, more than you can handle. Life gets overwhelming, and there seems to be no hope of getting out of the vicious cycle. I'm going to help you realize there is hope to break this cycle if only you will believe and trust in God.

Let's conduct a little test about trust. How many times have you approached a train crossing trusting that the crossing gate and lights are working? Do you ever come to a stop at the crossing if the lights aren't flashing or the guard isn't down? Of course you don't. But the components that make up a train crossing are run by sensors, computers, and motors. Technology fails. (I'll bet you slow down from now on.) If just one component fails, you could easily die. But when you put your trust in God, you never have to worry. Because God is not mechanical. He never fails you, and with your faith in Him, you will never die.

Pastor Matt Spangler, from the Evangelical Free Church of Canton, Illinois, my home church, took a few weeks of his sermons and spoke about everyday, common phrases that people "quote" from the Bible that just are not there. One of those phrases: "God won't give you more than you can handle." As Pastor Matt said: God didn't say that! While 1 Corinthians 10:13 does state "He will not let you be tempted beyond what you can bear," I look at this verse during the dark times in this way: God will always give you the needed help and comfort in the times in which you are overwhelmed. He will not take away those times.

He wants us to cry out to Him. He wants to be our Protector and Provider of comfort. During the depressive cycles, it is very hard to remember that God is ever-present. But we must have the faith and understanding that He will never leave us. Be faithful in prayer and praise to God, and He will hear your cries.

Paul also points out that when we are tempted God will provide a way out so we can endure it. But what does that even mean? What way out? The easy way? Those who struggle with depression know exactly what I mean when I say "the easy way." Self-harm to take away the pain present in this life. God never said life would be easy. God wants us to rely on Him and His presence in our lives. With this hope we can endure any storm. That is so hard to remember when the demons have overtaken our thoughts.

One of my biggest struggles is that I feel I am burdening others. Let's be honest: we often internalize struggles of nearly any kind. Whether you suffer from mental illness or not, daily challenges can affect even the strongest person. The feeling of being a burden is not confined to mental illness. However, I tend to take it to a much different level. My definition of a burden during the dark times means I should leave this world so I can save others from pain. In rational times, like now, as I write this, that just sounds ridiculous. But when the demons invade my mind, it sounds rational. It is a vicious circle of lies and deception versus reality.

Another challenge is how people perceive me. When I am struggling with my thoughts, I may come off as standoffish, rude, uninterested, or antisocial. I don't mean to, and it breaks my heart to think that people see me that way. When I become unstable, sometimes at the drop of a hat, all I can think about is how to get away. If I'm in public when it happens, I *have* to get away. Please understand that it's not you or anything that you said or did. It's a defense mechanism kicking in. To all of the people I have made feel this way, I am truly sorry.

I believe God has provided people and resources in our lives to provide a way out. Think about the fact that we have scientists to develop medicine to help with the effects of mental disorders. We have doctors to whom, I believe, God has given wisdom and patience so they can complete the schooling to help heal others. I certainly can't develop medicine or diagnose illness. Only God can make that happen, and we are blessed that He loves us that much.

I think back to all the times Satan has had a stronghold on me. Satan lives on deception, as seen in Genesis with Adam and Eve and the Tree of Life, and that type of deception can mean immediate despair to someone with a mental illness. One particular time stands out as a life or death moment to me. Back in early 2013, work wasn't going well. My boss at the time made it known that he was smarter than—and superior to—me. I started to believe it, and Satan reinforced it. He tried to convince me to give up and leave this world—and almost succeeded. But one morning, sitting at the kitchen table, I leaned on the strength of God to fight back against Satan. I prayed for intervention and looked for anything to bring me through the deadly cycle. I opened a book of devotions that I had been reading and saw three words: *You are worthy.* I felt a peace and understanding I hadn't felt in a very long time. Those three words saved my life that day. God is stronger, God is bigger, and God is love. God won the battle on my behalf. Satan was defeated on that day, but he certainly didn't give up.

I have family and friends who love me unconditionally and don't view me as a burden. But, most of all, I have a loving and faithful God who allows me to cry out to Him. All these factors allow me to wake each morning and do my best to chase the demons away. I'm not always immediately successful, but after that morning of God letting me know that I am worthy, I cling to those three words now more than ever. And always remember, you are worthy too.

I have a sign that my daughter put in the kitchen so that it is directly in my line of vision each morning. It says: "On particularly rough days when I'm sure I can't possibly endure, I like to remind myself that my track record for getting through bad days so far is 100 percent, and that's pretty good." This is an inspiration to me to not let the burdens of this world, or my mind, overtake my importance to God, family, and friends. In my opinion, Paul's primary message to the church at Corinth was not the fact that God won't give you more than you can handle, but instead an encouragement to stay faithful and know that God will hear your cries and give you comfort. Set your sights on Him, and He will provide peace and protect you no matter what life throws at you. You are not a burden. You are a child of God—and He will never leave you if you believe in His power and love.

My Prayer: God, thank you for another day on this earth, as it is one day closer to spending eternity with You. Please comfort me in my time of need and help me keep at bay the demons who want to overtake my mind. I know that I am not a burden to others and that they love me, and may I seek Your protection and comfort in the times I forget. I give You all the praise and glory in the good times and the bad. Thank you for loving me even in the times I don't love myself.

REFLECTIVE QUESTIONS

In what ways do you feel like a burden to others?

_____

_____

_____

_____

_____

In what things do you find comfort?

_____

_____

_____

_____

_____

Reflect again on 1 Corinthians 10:13. What is your prayer?

_____

_____

_____

_____

_____

Chapter 2

STRONG AND COURAGEOUS

JOSHUA 1:9

"Have I not commanded you? Be strong and coura-geous. Do not be afraid; Do not be discouraged; for the Lord, your God, will be with you wherever you go."

From the accounts of the book of Exodus, Joshua was one of two people left from the generation that left the enslavement of Egypt to find and enter Canaan, the Promised Land, the land God would provide. God spoke to Joshua after Moses died and told him that he was now to take up the cause to lead the people to the Promised Land so they might take possession of it. Joshua submitted to God's command and prepared himself to lead more than one million people across the Jordan River by having faith in God's direction.

He needed to be strong and have the courage to fulfill the mission in front of him. He relied on God to help him through.

As I read this verse, it reminds me there are times I need the courage and strength to travel from the dark times into the light God has promised me. That was the purpose of the Israelites reaching Canaan: to leave the shackles of Egypt behind and start anew in a land promised to them. It took faith by the people—in God, and Joshua—for that to happen. After forty years of wandering in the wilderness, a new generation had emerged from the people that had only heard the stories of their ancestors being slaves in Egypt. Joshua and Caleb were the only two people left who had firsthand knowledge of the suffering of the Israelite people and what God had done to free them from their shackles. God had listened to and answered the prayers of the people when they cried out. The Israelites had to be reminded that God had not left them and would provide for them if they would only ask for His help.

God commanded Moses, and then Joshua, to be strong and courageous in their journey. To not fear the unknown because He was with them. How many times have you wondered what happened to your strength and courage when you were in the throes of mental anguish? During a depressive cycle, I am beaten down and scared because of the irrational thoughts

I'm having. These thoughts are far from God's command in Joshua 1:9. For God to say things like "Be strong; be courageous; don't be afraid; don't be discouraged" are extremely hard to reconcile when demons have overtaken my thoughts. I *am* afraid. I *am* discouraged. And I am *not* strong and courageous.

Do you ever think these same thoughts went through the minds of the people of Israel or, for that matter, Joshua and Caleb themselves? Of course they did. They were flawed just like we are; Joshua and Caleb were not perfect people. Sin entered the world in Genesis chapter 3 and that began the path for the plan of salvation through Jesus Christ. There is only one perfect person who has ever walked this earth who was sinless, and now He sits at the right hand of God in Heaven. Joshua is not that person, so his faith certainly waned throughout his journey.

The key to this verse, in my eyes, is the fact that God will never leave us. His command is clear, but what you don't see is a "you will" in His commands. (In other words, this is not in the context of an absolute statement such as "you will die." We know that will happen at some point. That is an absolute statement.) So what does this mean? It means God didn't tell us that we absolutely, positively won't encounter times that we challenge God's authority and direction. You don't see: "you *will*" be strong and courageous; "you *will*" not be afraid; "you *will*" not be discouraged.

God continually reminds us that He commanded us to do these things. These weren't directives that He knew we would follow instantly. This is because we are flawed, sinful people. He wants us to look to Him in times of trouble. He wants us to lean on Him when we are weak and afraid. To "be strong" is not necessarily physical strength; it means to be strong of mind. God will give us that strength even though, at times, it is hidden. We just need to have faith and trust in Him.

There is no doubt that our mind fails at times. With that, our faith in God fails at times as well. But God has promised us that He will never fail us. Because of our human flaws, he needs to remind us from time to time that He is waiting for us to recognize Him again. This can certainly take time depending on the moment.

My depressive cycles take on a form of their own and are so unpredictable. The triggers are not always defined. Imagine being stable one second and irrational the next. Nothing really happened. I'm just going down the road to despair with no brakes. God doesn't do anything to stop the out-of-control journey down the dark mountain. He waits to see if you are going to call on Him to provide the stopping point. It doesn't mean we won't crash; it means God will protect us from being injured too severely. We will walk away from the crash because God has put His hand of protection in front of a spiraling situation.

One of my favorite activities has always been going to St. Louis Cardinals games. Being part of the crowd always invigorated me. Baseball is my favorite pastime, and being part of Cardinals Nation came naturally to me. But over the years I have learned that I can't expose myself to large crowds. While most triggers are hard to define or predict, I realized that too much noise and being in a crowd of people are definite triggers for me. I can't focus, and I dread the very thing that made me so happy in the past.

We always caught the Metrolink in Collinsville, Illinois to travel to Busch Stadium. As we got closer to the stadium, more people got on the train. As the train became more full, the more my anxiety took over. I was so excited to go to the game, but as more and more people surrounded me, the excitement went away. I couldn't breathe. I couldn't stop the noise. I went from stable to irrational in a matter of minutes. Once we got to the stadium, I couldn't even enjoy the game. All I could think about was getting back on a train full of people—people shoving, pushing, and talking loudly. Everything would fall in around me. I prayed for it to stop, but it just didn't. I knew after just a few times of this that my days of being part of the excitement in the stadium were over.

I'd love to say that, when the demons invade, my thoughts go immediately to God. That is just not the case. It is one of my human failures, and I completely own it. In a rational mind, I always wonder why I can't just give it up to Him at the beginning of the cycle. I am trying so hard to get the voices to stop and find the internal strength to stop the spiral myself. The flawed part of that strategy is: "I". *I* am trying to stop the voices. *I* am trying to find the strength. God is waiting for us to ask for help in the battle.

Think of it this way. As a child, when we are afraid or hurt, we seek our parents for comfort, healing, and protection. It is no different being a child of God. He knows that you will eventually run to Him for all that comforts you. He anticipates it; He even longs for it. Just as we get in a spiral and realize there are no brakes to stop our descent down the dark road, He reminds us that there is safety in Him if we will just cry out. Have faith in Him that He will stop you from certain death and put you on the right path to safety and comfort. He did that for Moses, Joshua, and the Israelite people when He freed all Israel from certain death and showed them the path to the land He promised them. He put His hand of protection above the people and led them to the light. If we ask for the same protection and direction in our life, God will provide that light.

Reflective Questions

In what ways do you battle, or stand in, the darkness?

_____

_____

_____

_____

_____

How do you need God to bring light to that darkness?

_____

_____

_____

_____

_____

Based on Joshua 1:9, what is your prayer? How will you ask God to help you be strong and courageous, to bring light to your darkness?

_____

_____

_____

_____

_____

Chapter 3

JOY OVER ANXIETY

Philippians 4:6, 7

"Do not be anxious about anything but in every situation, by prayer and petition, with thanksgiving, present your requests to God. And the peace of God, which transcends all understanding, will guard your hearts and minds in Jesus Christ."

Paul wrote the book of Philippians to the Christians in the city of Philippi while he was imprisoned in Rome. His purpose was to give hope to all Christians by reinforcing that true joy could be found if they continued to share the Good News to all who would hear. That joy, in fact, was the promise of eternal life through the blood that was spilled for them on the cross. The joy of knowing their sins had been forgiven and Jesus was preparing a place for them in Heaven. Philippians 4:4

says, *"Rejoice in the Lord always. I will say it again: Rejoice!"* Paul goes on to tell them how to approach joy and peace in their earthly life with the anticipation of spending eternity with Jesus.

Joy means something different to everybody. Joy can be winning the lottery. Joy can be becoming a spouse, parent, or grandparent. Joy can be getting that new car you've been saving for. Joy can be finally coming out of a cycle in which it felt as though the demons would never let go. These are all earthly joys that are self-focused and not God-focused. Please note: I am not saying you are selfish by enjoying earthly possessions. That is human nature in all of us. But don't forget to put God first in your joy. After all, He is the reason that we have what we have. All you have to do is read the Psalms to see true, God-focused joy. David wrote, or can be attributed to have written, 73 of the 150 Psalms. In Psalms 100:1-3, you can feel the love for the Lord and joy in David's heart: *"Shout for joy to the Lord, all the earth. Worship the Lord with gladness; come before Him with joyful songs. Know that the Lord is God."* How powerful is that? David, with all of his challenges in life, understood that no matter how dark his life became, he still knew the joy that God had presented to him—and he openly praised God for it. Joy to the Lord is hard to fathom in times of despair. Just as David strayed from God at times, we too must remember that when the darkness moves in,

God doesn't leave us. He is patiently waiting for us to shout to Him in joy during the good times. He comforts us and hears our cries of despair just as loudly as our cries of joy. Allow Him in your life in times of trouble just as in times of peace. He is listening and He will act. Allow Him time and you will see His glory.

The Lord Jesus Christ came to this earth to spread the word of eternal life. Who wouldn't be joyous about that? Paul was telling the people of Philippi to not be anxious. However, did you catch the "but" in the Philippians 4 passage? Paul knew that, while the directive is clear, as earthly people we will be anxious about various aspects of our life. He knew it took faith in Christ to understand that one day we will no longer be anxious in His physical presence.

Anxiety is part of my daily life. There are triggers I know will cause anxiety, such as being in a group of people and many voices speaking at once, but there are also unknown triggers. I have finally reached the point in which I can recognize most of the early onset of panic attacks and remove myself from those situations. But in cases where the attacks come unexpectedly, I must remember to breathe and cry out to God. That is not always easy, but it is effective if I stay calm and focused. I will discuss more about my anxiety and panic attacks later, but for now suffice it to say that I try my best to remember this verse in times of panic and times of joy.

I believe I am a poster child for taking the smallest situation and turning it into the tallest mountain. I text my wife, Jeanine, every night as I leave work. If I don't get an immediate text back, I begin to worry. What if she's hurt? What if I made her mad? What if she has left me? *What if she is having an affair?* See? Irrational. But as I stated earlier, she is my rock. My center. I fear that at some point she will say enough is enough. Now, she will tell me that that is an unrealistic fear—but it is my fear nonetheless. This is a daily fear that really has nothing to do with the disorder. When you love someone so deeply and rely on them to keep you stable, the thought of losing that is more than you can bear. I can't imagine my life without her. She knows just the right thing to say at the perfect time.

Now do me a favor. Go back and reread the previous paragraph and replace Jeanine/she with God/Him. (Outside of the whole affair thing, of course.) Why can't we love God with this same tenacity and passion?

I wish I had the ability to always turn my anxieties and worries into prayer. As hard as I try, I sometimes forget. Does God turn His back on me when I have a moment that I am not crying out to Him? Of course not. Does He think I have lost all my faith in Him? Nope. He waits for me to realize that I am trying to deal with the situation myself. Who wouldn't want a little extra help in times of worry? Especially from someone who created the universe in six days! He will not forsake me in a moment of weakness just because I don't immediately pray to Him. I'm pretty sure God is used to that!

I've been known to say "Oops! Sorry, God!" when my focus went to me and not Him. I can picture Him in Heaven smiling at me to let me know it's okay. At least I came back to Him eventually, and that is all that matters. We all have times of weakness when we completely focus on ourselves. It's okay. Don't let that add to your anxiety and stress.

Paul did his best to give the directive from God in the Philippians 4 passage, but I really believe that he knew, somewhere deep within his faith, that we needed a little more guidance with the command. Why else would he put the "but" in his statement? Just as Paul recognized the need to expand the statement, we must always remember there may be a "but." God will hear you and act accordingly to be your Protector and Comforter, even if it isn't immediately evident or you aren't immediately focusing on Him.

We all backslide and walk away. It may take some time to come back, but God will wait. He knows your story and knows that you have strayed from the path. But once the joy comes back and the anxiety subsides, He will be ready to walk with you again.

REFLECTIVE QUESTIONS

What are some of the true joys in your life?

_____

_____

_____

_____

_____

In what situations do you find yourself being anxious?

_____

_____

_____

_____

_____

Read Philippians 4:6, 7 once more. Based on that passage, what is your prayer?

_____

_____

_____

_____

_____

PART II

HOPE

Chapter 4

A HOPE AND A FUTURE

JEREMIAH 29:11

"For I know the plans I have for you, declares the Lord. Plans to prosper you and not harm you. Plans to give you hope and a future."

Jeremiah was known as "the weeping prophet." Poor Jeremiah. No one listened to him. He was God's spokesman to Judah for forty years. Throughout the book that bears his name, he was thrown in prison, thrown in a cistern, and taken to Egypt against his will. He was rejected by his friends, family, neighbors, priests, and many other people. Jeremiah was trying to get Judah and Jerusalem to repent of their sins and turn their focus back to God. His voice went unheard. He wept for the country he loved so much. He was considered a failure by the people, but God considered him one of his most successful prophets because of his obedience and faithfulness.

How many times have you felt rejected? It can be something as small as not being accepted into a group in school or as large as people disassociating themselves from you because of your mental illness. I've experienced both. In high school, I wasn't a jock. I wasn't a nerd. I wasn't in the band, nor was I a star athlete. I referred to myself as "medium." That seemed to be the theme of my life. Just . . . medium. I never excelled at anything, but I wasn't horribly bad at anything either. I was just the center stripe of the road.

I worked way too hard to be accepted. I wanted to be part of something. But no matter how hard I tried, I just wasn't part of any clique. So I forced my way into a clique that would accept me. I turned to alcohol and drugs. Not hard drugs; just marijuana and speed. These days, the drugs on the streets are much more powerful and addictive. Where I live, methamphetamines, or meth for short, is a very dangerous, highly addictive drug. In the '80s, speed gave you endless energy. Now meth can kill you. (I did try acid once, but it wasn't for me. I saw a Siamese cat flying a kite in a thunderstorm. I'm pretty sure a cat can't fly a kite. At least, my cats can't. I knew at that moment: I would stick with pot, speed, and alcohol.)

I didn't know God back then. I couldn't have cared less for God. My main goal in life was to drink as much as I could and smoke more pot than anyone else. I started with beer and progressed to whiskey. I could drink a fifth of whiskey and smoke more than an ounce of pot a night. There were seven to ten of us in a group that would pool everyone's money to buy all the alcohol, pot, and speed we could. It was usually from the lunch money our parents gave us, but there were a couple of people who had part-time jobs to supplement our habit. I finally found a group I could fit in with. We all had a common goal of drinking and smoking ourselves into oblivion. No judgment. No shame.

I look back now and wonder how I ever survived that phase. It lasted from when I was 15 until I met Jeanine at 20. Let me rephrase that: I look back now and know that God had a purpose for me in this life. There were so many times I don't even remember driving home. God protected me from myself and the people I could have killed driving drunk or high. God put Jeanine in my life as a voice of maturity and love that I had never experienced before. Jeanine is six years older than me (sorry, honey). She had survived so many challenges in life. She was exactly the person God wanted me to be with for so many reasons. Jeanine saved my life from going into an abyss I never would have gotten out of. But God saved my life so that, eventually, I would find and follow Him. He already knows the path of our life and every mistake or trial that will happen. He will reveal these things to you in His time. Until then He will protect you so you can one day be a vessel for His glory.

He had plans for me just as He had plans for Jeremiah. He kept pushing Jeremiah to continue to spread His message even though Jeremiah was continually rejected by everyone around him. But, as stated in the verse atop this chapter, He also has plans for me to prosper. To give me hope and a future. Had I stayed on the road I was on in my younger years, I truly believe, at some point, it would have killed me and I would have spent eternity in Hell. But God, and Jeanine, gave me a new path, one in which I would prosper. Keep in mind, God giving you a plan to prosper you doesn't mean He is going to make you rich or give you a dream life. It means you will prosper for Him. He never promises that you won't go through tough times in life, but if you stay faithful to Him, He gives us unlimited hope.

My challenges with Bipolar Disorder have tested my faith to the depths of my soul. To have to deal with suicidal thoughts is hypocritical to living a Christian life. At church, I praise God in so many ways. I feel the Holy Spirit in our worship music, our prayer time, and when Pastor Matt delivers his message. I sometimes deal with concentration issues while at church, but I can honestly say that I've never had a suicidal thought during our services. I give all the glory to God for that.

During the worst cycles, I struggle to understand how God can feel so far away. In church I have faith that God is ever-present. Away from church, I've cursed the absence of God in my life. I find myself doing or thinking things that contradict all that I know as a Christian. Everything that I believe and know is right is overshadowed by irrational thoughts of hopelessness and despair and the feeling that God has abandoned me. This is probably my biggest challenge and certainly the largest test of my faith. Every one of the feelings are real and raw until I come out of the cycle. That is when the true test of my faith begins. Do I continue my sinful ways or refocus my energy on God? It always seems like God finds a way to let me know He is in control and that I need to refocus on Him after the cycle is over. It may be a passage of Scripture, a podcast I'm listening to, or something I read in a devotional. God always seems to say the right things as long as I am willing to listen. He's perfect like that.

Sometimes hope seems so far away, as I'm sure it did with Jeremiah. I have to choose to have hope every single day. One reminder is the tattoo on my right forearm, in my wife's handwriting, that says "Hope." There is also a semicolon after it. A semicolon is used when a writer chooses to continue a thought even though a sentence could end at that point. The symbolism of a semicolon in the mental illness community is that we could choose to end our story but we make the conscious effort to continue. At the end of the day, I know that the largest hope I have every day is the chance of eternal life through the blood that was shed by His Son for the forgiveness of sin.

We all sin, but there are times in our life when it seems we sin more than others. Remember, a sin is a sin. Asking forgiveness for that sin by asking Jesus into your heart wipes the slate clean. He took the sins of the world on Himself for all people: past, present, and future. He is the Alpha and Omega, the Beginning and the End. We will continue to sin because we are human. But the difference is that God forgives the sinner who reaches out to Him.

The sins of my youth were, at times, beyond comprehension. I didn't know God. What a joyous day, in 2000, when God spoke to my heart—even after all the awful times of my youth—and led me to His Son. I now have the anticipation of spending eternity in Heaven, and the even greater anticipation of Jesus greeting me with open arms, saying, "Well done, good and faithful servant." At least, that is my hope.

REFLECTIVE QUESTIONS

What are some experiences when you felt rejected, and how did you get through those times?

_____

_____

_____

_____

_____

Have you asked Jesus into your heart? If you have, how has your life changed since that happened?

_____

_____

_____

_____

_____

With Jeremiah 29:11 in mind, what is your prayer?

_____

_____

_____

_____

_____

Chapter 5

PRESENT SUFFERING

ROMANS 8:18

"I consider that our present sufferings are not worth comparing with the glory that will be revealed to us."

Paul prepared the message to the Romans, while in Corinth, as a precursor to his arrival in Rome. Neither he nor any of the other apostles had been to Rome to visit the church formed by the Jews after Pentecost as described at the beginning of Acts chapter 2. During Pentecost, Jews from many nations had gathered at one of the great annual festivals. *"Suddenly a sound like the blowing of a violent wind came from Heaven and filled where they were sitting. . . . All of them were filled with the Holy Spirit and began to speak in other tongues as the Spirit enabled them"* (Acts 2:2, 4). All in attendance were confused, but they did realize something supernatural was happening. They wanted an explanation. Peter stepped forward and explained the truth about God.

How cool would it be to be like Peter and take the time to explain the truth and glory of God? I remember early in my walk with the Lord. I was on fire for God! I wanted to talk to anyone who would listen about how God transformed my life even though the sins of my past were great. God chose to love me even though I shunned Him for years. And now I was reborn in Jesus—that was such a glorious feeling!

By nature, I am scientific in my thinking. I don't believe in most conspiracy theories. I must be presented with true, hard facts of a situation. (I believe the Holocaust actually happened, that a man truly did walk on the moon, and that 9/11 was an act of cowardice terrorism from a foreign country not precipitated by the United States.) It was a great step for me to have faith in something I had not researched thoroughly prior to believing it. But the Holy Spirit came into my heart with such passion and love that my scientific mind accepted it without question. I, like Peter, stepped up and told people about God without reservation. God's Word was all the research I needed.

No one told me that once you accept Christ into your heart you will still go through trials. That there will be sadness, anger, questions, complete and utter loss of faith, and so much more. They didn't teach those things in my New Christians class shortly after I accepted Christ. I expected roses and rainbows for the rest of my life because God had forgiven me and was now the main focus of my life. So there I was, telling all the world about God—and there were still areas of my life I felt were crumbling around me.

Why wasn't God helping me with my struggles? Honestly, as I look back at 2000 and early 2001, this may have been the first sign of having some type of mental disorder. My mind raced constantly. I had a very difficult time concentrating even on minimal tasks. Sometimes, just trying to function daily was such a challenge and, at other times, my concentration level was right on point. I believe now that my brain was starting to fail me. It would be another decade or so before I was officially diagnosed, but there was certainly something happening. How many times do we just write these types of moments off to being busy, working too hard, or overloaded from all directions? That certainly can be the case, but I realized many years later that it was much deeper than that.

I've come to realize that Romans 8:18 encapsulates so much of my faith. I do suffer daily, and usually silently, so as not to burden others. People talk about aspects of mental illness as being about selfishness. What is selfish, to me, is feeling like I am a burden to others. I'm not the best at outwardly expressing my true feelings when I am going through a cycle. It may show in my facial expressions or one-on-one interactions, but I try to contain that. There are times I feel like I'm in a microwave. I am getting hot from the inside out. All of the burning anxiety, hopelessness, and self-worth issues that I struggle with so much are starting so deep inside me and never fully reaching the surface. This is *my* present suffering.

I deal with all the "self" feelings: self-worth, self-esteem, self-pity, self-image. The list goes on. Add all this on top of anxious situations, feelings of despair, and thoughts of suicide. Even as I write this chapter on this particular day, I keep asking myself if I am worthy to write this book. I pray deeply that God speaks through me with each keystroke. I want my message to be clear, and not repetitive, so people can receive the ultimate message of the glory of God shining through my life even during the darkest times. God, by contrast, is repetitive in my life, but in a very good way: in the way that he loves me and protects me every single day. Without that hope, my days would be even darker.

Paul's message to the Jews in Rome was clear: believe in the power of Jesus Christ with all your strength, all your heart, and all your soul. This will reveal the glory of God when we leave this earth. Our suffering now will be eliminated later in the presence of the Lord in Heaven. As the demons attack our minds, God will not fail us. He is ever-present. He knows our struggles and daily battles of faith. He knows that we will ask "Why?" He hears our "self" issues. All He requires is that we ultimately remember who is in control.

Our book of life has been written and, just as in Revelation, Jesus reinforces that He is the Alpha and the Omega, the Beginning and the End. I have that phrase tattooed on my left shoulder as a reminder that His suffering on the cross far outweighs my daily struggles. He withstood unthinkable beatings, ridicule, and being nailed to the cross for the forgiveness of sin for all who believe.

To me, this is scientific truth as told in the Bible. Jesus' death and resurrection were prophesied many times in the Old Testament. Isaiah 53:3-5 is ever-present with me: *"He was despised and rejected by mankind, a man of suffering, and familiar with pain. Surely he took up our pain and bore our suffering, yet we considered him punished by God, stricken by him, and afflicted. But he was pierced for our transgressions and he was crushed for our iniquities, and the punishment that brought us peace was on him. And by his wounds, we are healed."*

Isaiah knew the fate of Jesus even before the Messiah was born. My present suffering doesn't hold a candle to those types of suffering. I have faith that the glory of God will be revealed to us one day in Heaven. What a glorious day that will be.

REFLECTIVE QUESTIONS

What are some ways you reveal the glory of God to others?

_____

_____

_____

_____

_____

What are some frustrations you encounter while doing so?

_____

_____

_____

_____

_____

Think through Romans 8:18 once more. What is your prayer?

_____

_____

_____

_____

_____

Chapter 6

OVERCOMING FEAR

Isaiah 41:10

"Do not fear, for I am with you. Do not be dismayed,
for I am your God. I will strengthen you and help you.
I will uphold you with my righteous right hand."

Isaiah was probably the greatest prophet in the Bible. In Isaiah's day, priests and prophets had a valuable place in continuing the education of God and spreading the word of God's wrath and judgment to the people. Priests speak to God on behalf of the people. Prophets speak to people on behalf of God, and it was Isaiah's job to relay the Word of God to the people of Judah and reign them in after they had strayed. He warned them of God's wrath and punishment if they didn't change their sinful ways. As you can imagine, his judgment of Judah on behalf of God didn't sit well with the people. But Isaiah, who reflected God and His message in glorious ways, not only wanted the people of Judah to reflect on their sins, he also prophesied to the people the coming of a Messiah.

I have times when I feel so alone. I feel as though I am the only person who suffers from a mental illness. The demons take over my thoughts and try to get me to believe that not only am I alone in my earthly life, God has also abandoned me. While this doesn't seem rational, it is very real at the moment. I'm not sure there are any more extreme feelings when combined with being alone and in despair. You are fooled into thinking that the whole world is crumbling around you. But what is really happening in this: Satan is trying to turn you away from God. Satan wants you to think God has abandoned you. Of course, nothing could be further from the truth, but when you are in that moment of despair and loneliness, you listen to everything your mind is telling you. This makes for a dangerous crossroad.

In the account recorded in Genesis chapter 3, sin entered the world. In my study Bible, the heading of Genesis 3 is "The Fall." It is when Satan, described as the serpent, is in the garden with Adam and Eve that he asks Eve, *"Did God really say you must not eat from any tree in the garden?"* (Genesis 3:1) This is the beginning of the fall of man through which sin, if left of its own accord, leads to eternity in Hell. But soon after, in the recorded account of Genesis chapter 12, the plan of salvation through Jesus Christ is set into action through Abraham's bloodline. Satan convinced Eve (in Genesis 3) that it was okay to eat the fruit of the Tree of Knowledge of Good and Evil. This is no different than Satan and his demons taking over our minds to tell us there is no hope and we are alone in our struggles. Just as he deceived Eve, Satan hopes to deceive us so we disown God and all the strength He provides us in times of trouble.

The prophet Isaiah spoke to the people, and what he said still holds true for us today. He sought to remind the Israelites that no matter what Satan throws at us, we should not be dismayed or fear the unknown because God is with us. He will give us the strength to take on any challenge. I find myself, in the dark times, asking for God's help, asking Him to be with me. I also find myself screaming in my head for the demons to go away. During thoughts of suicide, I cry out *Stop, stop, STOP!* over and over in my head. I'm trying to get the darkness and despair to leave. I truly believe God hears that cry and takes on the battles with the demons for me. Even though I may not specifically cry out to God at that time, He becomes my strength at the perfect time.

I am trying to get the demons to stop. He has the power to get the demons to stop. He has fought these battles with Satan before and knows exactly what to do. God's power is greater than all other powers. It's certainly greater than mine. While I tend to be a bit of a control freak, I have learned that it's okay to be vulnerable and let God fight on my behalf.

There are days I fail to thank Him for all the promises and love He gives me. Those tend to be the days Satan and his demons have overtaken my every thought. But I know and truly believe that God is fighting my battles—often without my even recognizing it—until a time when the demons are driven away and my focus goes back to Him. That means I have to give up control in my life and ask Him to take over.

How often have we tried to control a situation that we clearly should have given to God? Answer: try every day. Whether it be my very long drive to work, my finances, my family life, or any other situation that is consuming my thoughts, God is always in control. But as an imperfect human, I want control. Can I stop a deer from running out in front of me? Or an unexpected repair to my home or vehicle? Or a serious life event within my family? Absolutely not—but I sure want to. This is not what God wants from us. I heard a saying once that what consumes your mind controls your life. So let's try this: let God consume your mind so that He controls your life. Not so easy to do, right? At least not for me, especially when I am in a depressive cycle. But let's get away from filling our minds with all the negative thoughts and focus on the love, protection, and promises given to us by Him. He is not going to fix everything based on our timeline, but I promise you that you will find more peace giving your worries—and especially control—over to Him.

Isaiah tells me that God will uphold me with His righteous right hand. In the book that bears his name, there is no doubt that, seated in God's right hand, we need not fear anything in this life. He makes it very clear that He is with me, He has established His love for me, He will take away all fear because He will be strong for us, and He will send a Messiah to take away our sins so Satan doesn't pull us down with him. Faith and control. Have faith in our God that He is always in control. Those are such hard concepts to grasp, but in faith, they are the foundations of my daily activities.

I try not to take advantage of God and His power. I don't want Him to only take on the battle when the demons are around. I want Him to battle for me every second of every day. In my life, the battle is not easy. My sins are great and my focus isn't always on Him. But He fights with such love and compassion that I might not suffer in this world, and He is continually reminding me that the end of the race will be won once I reach Heaven and have eternal life through Jesus Christ.

It's a marathon, not a sprint. I have to train every day to ensure I have the endurance to finish the race.

And through His righteous right hand, I have all I need to persevere.

REFLECTIVE QUESTIONS

In what ways can you allow God to strengthen you?

_____

_____

_____

_____

_____

What are the training tools you need to finish the race?

_____

_____

_____

_____

_____

Reread Isaiah 41:10. Based on that verse, what is your prayer?

_____

_____

_____

_____

_____

PART III

LOVE

Chapter 7

THE STRUGGLE: LESSONS FROM PAUL

2 Timothy 1:7
"For the spirit of God gave us does not make us timid but gives us power, love, and self-discipline."

Paul was facing death in a Roman prison. He was convicted under Emperor Nero for being a follower of Jesus Christ. Paul took his time in prison to send a letter to Timothy, who was a leader of the church in Ephesus. Paul looked to Timothy as a son, and also as the one who would continue to spread the Gospel of Jesus Christ after Paul's execution. Not only did Paul give Timothy instructions on how to continue his ministry, he also provided him warnings against the opposition and nonbelievers Timothy would encounter along the way. Paul loved Timothy. Paul was motivated by a deep love for Timothy the person and for his continuing quest to hold true the teachings of salvation.

Paul was a man of deep faith with a tenacious conviction for Christ. He died alone in a Roman prison, but his spirit continued to live through his "son," Timothy.

As I sit here today I am troubled. I feel so far from God. I have days like this, days in which I don't feel worthy of Jesus' love or the sacrifice He made for me. I told myself I wouldn't write unless I was in the frame of mind to glorify God and acknowledge all the blessings He has bestowed on me. But even though I am struggling today, I felt led to put this exact period of time in this book. The slightest hint of things not going as planned gets escalated, in my mind, into the world coming down around me.

I didn't go to church yesterday. I didn't feel up to interacting with people. I needed quiet time to collect myself and bring my focus back to God. But that hasn't come yet. I had hoped that I would get out my Bible and begin to type with the expectation that the Holy Spirit would come to me in my time of trouble. I'm hoping this time of writing gets my mind, body, and soul back in line with God. I'm hoping God hears my cries and settles my mind.

But those things haven't come yet.

I can't imagine being in Paul's shoes knowing you are about to be executed for loving Jesus. There wasn't a question of *if* Paul was going to die—just when. Even though he knew his time of bringing nonbelievers to Christ was over, he still loved God with such passion that his only thought was making sure Timothy was equipped to continue the message of salvation. Paul knew his earthly death meant spending eternity in the Kingdom of God. But I'm sure he was still scared. He put all of that aside, however, to ensure that his message continued.

I sit here wondering why I can't put all of my angst aside and refocus on God. I hate the feeling of being so far from where I need to be. I agonize over the decisions I have made. Jesus himself agonized over what He knew was going to happen. Jesus went to the Mount of Olives with His disciples and withdrew from them to pray. *"'Father, if you are willing, take this cup from me; yet not my will but yours be done.' An angel from heaven appeared before him and strengthened him. And being in anguish, he prayed more earnestly and his sweat was like drops of blood falling to the ground"* (Luke 22:42-44).

I could surely use an angel from Heaven to strengthen me today. But with or without one, I know I need to continue to focus on God and His never-ending love for me. Just as Jesus prayed in earnest, so will I. For

God's love is eternal, and even in times of despair, He is there to love and protect us.

Even though I know this is a cycle and it will end, it's hard to do what I know is right. My prayer today is for God to stay with me as I work through my struggles. I pray for the demons to leave my mind so I can get back to glorifying God. His love shines on me even though my focus is somewhere else. I just need to keep praying for an end to this cycle and that His will be done in my life. He has a purpose for me, and I want to continue that journey with Him.

God had a purpose for Paul, too, and Paul fulfilled that purpose until the time of his death. That is a level of love for God that I crave. I often wonder about my disorder, if that time will ever come, a time when I completely and unconditionally give up my life to Him, just as Paul did. In times of neutral emotions, I would like to think I accomplish that. But in times like today, everything just reminds me that I still have a lot of work to do. I was hoping that by the end of this chapter the demons would stop and all my thoughts would have turned to God. That hasn't happened. But I will continue to fight and pray for God's love and mercy so that my story can continue.

He still has a job for me to accomplish, and I will not give in to the demons. Always remember that you need to continue to fight even in the worst of days.

God still loves you no matter what you are feeling. That is my hope, my reason for living.

Tomorrow will be a better day.

Postscript: I wrote this chapter during a three-day weekend in which I struggled the entire time. As I update this chapter, I am now in a better frame of mind. I gave serious thought to eliminating the content and starting over. However, I have prayed about it, and I feel you should see how raw the emotions and cycles really can be. What I want you to take from this chapter is not only the love of God but His faithfulness to remain with us even in times of despair. I look back on what I wrote and realize that I came through this cycle with my eyes focused on God and—because of Him and Him alone—the demons were kept at bay. With each cycle, I become stronger in my daily battle, and my love for God deepens.

REFLECTIVE QUESTIONS

How can you be more like Paul?

_____

_____

_____

_____

_____

What person, or persons, in your life can you help equip with the goal of continuing the message, just as Paul did with Timothy?

_____

_____

_____

_____

_____

Have you had a struggle that seemed like utter despair, but you came out stronger because of it? Write about that time.

_____

_____

_____

_____

_____

Chapter 8

SUSI

Colossians 3:12-14
"Therefore, as God's chosen people, holy and dearly loved, clothe yourself with compassion, kindness, humility, gentleness, and patience. Bear with each other and forgive one another if any of you have a grievance against someone. Forgive as the Lord forgave you. And over all these virtues put on love, which binds them all together in perfect unity."

Paul was in prison in Rome when he wrote the letter to the Colossians. (This was an imprisonment before the letter to Timothy referred to in the previous chapter.) His purpose was to quell the errors taking place within the church and convince the believers they had everything they needed in Christ. I am still amazed at the faithfulness Paul had in the face of death. The transition from Saul to Paul is an amazing story of transformation and is described in the book of Acts. Saul persecuted Christians; Paul loved the Lord with every part of his being. Saul encountered Jesus on the road to Damascus, and his earthly and eternal life was changed forever. Jesus had a purpose for Paul, and it wasn't only to continue the message given to us by Christ, it was for Paul to lay out the "rules" of living a Christian life. As written in his letter to the Colossians, over all of the Christian virtues it is love that binds everything together.

Once again, I want to be very real in this chapter. A huge struggle for me is that I hold grudges. If I have been wronged by someone, I will pretty much write that person off. There are times in my life when I give people too many chances. I try to see the good in them and think they will change. Sometimes a positive change happens. I reflect on how easy it would have been for me to walk away from that person without looking back. But something told me to give this person a chance to make it right, that they would not disappoint me. And by the grace of God they didn't. At other times I hang onto the hope that the person will change for the better, and yet they continue to use me for their gain. These are the times I just need to walk away to avoid further pain. The stress and anxiety that they cause are more detrimental to my mental well-being than the continued hope that they will change. So . . . I'm done with them.

My sister Sue was an alcoholic. She began drinking heavily in her late teens after losing her fiancé in a house fire. Alcohol was her coping mechanism. As I got into my mid-teens, I began to drink too. Not as a coping mechanism, but, as stated earlier, for the purpose for being accepted in a group. The two worlds collided when I reached my late teens. Susi and I hung out together with various people who liked to drink a lot. I found myself drinking almost every night at Susi's apartment. Most people like to get together on the weekends, and they might have a party that they regret the next day. Susi and I partied with the same group of people every night—people I didn't have school or work with, and so I would have zero regrets the next day. At that time I couldn't have cared less about the Lord or how to live a Christian life. I just wanted to get drunk, live a promiscuous life, and do it all over again the next day. I was lost, and so was Susi.

Though I didn't know it at the time, God had a plan for me. As I reflect on that period of my life, every situation in which I turned farther away from God made me a stronger Christian when I accepted Christ into my life. I can use my story to tell others—and they may or may not turn away from that life. I was not raised in a church where I could relate to all the people trying to find their way. Trying to find a purpose for their life. Trying to find hope in a dark place.

After accepting Christ into my heart, I tried to be a living example to Susi that there *is* a way to find peace in your heart without turning to the bottle. But it didn't work. After years of helping her financially, lovingly, spiritually, bailing her out of jail, and out of very bad situations on a consistent basis, I turned my back on her.

In 2012, my niece Allyson was entrusted to our care by the Illinois Department of Children and Family Services. Susi just could not take care of her anymore. I was so mad at Susi for not providing a life for Ally and her brother, Matt. I could handle all the times that Susi hurt me, but not taking care of her children was, in my mind, unforgivable. So Ally came to live with us, and I had Susi sign guardianship papers to ensure Ally was protected by us until she turned 18. Matt went his own way and had no desire to live with us or my other sister, Lori. I never stopped Susi from visiting Ally, but she rarely came around. In the short time after she came to us, Ally went from being our niece to being our daughter. It wasn't an easy transition, but Jeanine did such a great job showing Ally love and discipline by setting boundaries Ally never had before. It was like trying to tame a wild stallion into a trail horse. It took time, patience, and love—all of which I struggled with because of my bitterness against Susi.

I thank God daily for Ally and for Jeanine, who loved that broken child as if she were her own.

Susi passed away in 2013. She died from the culmination of all the years of abuse. She was living with a friend she had met in a recovery group. Susi painted the picture that her entire family had turned their backs on her, that she had nowhere to go. She convinced her friend that she was clean and sober but that we would still not accept her back into the family. She also told her friend that I had taken her child away from her.

Sue passed away in her sleep on her friend's couch. When we went to claim her belongings, a bottle of vodka was found under the couch cushions, and it was three-quarters gone. Her friend began to realize she had been manipulated too. She was trying to show love and understanding to my sister in a troubling time in her life. But Susi was so broken that the only way for her to cope with life was to drink and take advantage of other people. It was her survival instinct.

I now have to live with the burden of turning my back on my sister. When I read Colossians and all the directions Paul gives us for leading a Christian life, I know I fell short in a lot of areas with my sister. Early on I tried to show compassion, kindness, gentleness, patience, and love. Over time, with each lie that she told, those traits went away. As my disorder progressed, I used it to justify my feelings and actions toward Susi. I just couldn't get my mind focused on God for His help in dealing with the situation. I tried to handle it alone.

I can't change the past, but if I was given one more opportunity with Susi, I would want to encourage her to go to church with me every week. Even if it meant that I would have to drive to pick her up. I wouldn't have taken no for an answer. Maybe, just maybe, we could have studied Colossians together. Maybe reading Paul's charge to live and love as Christ did would have been the turning point in our relationship. I could have explained to her that I too had demons; they just took a different form. I took the position of God in her life. I judged her for her sins, and *my* wrath was to turn my back on her. Maybe if I had been in the Word more I could have changed our relationship and, in turn, she might have chosen to walk with God as I did. But I made an awful mistake and took my focus away from God and tried to fix the situation myself.

In Matthew 19:26 Jesus tells us that with God all things are possible. In Colossians, Paul gives us the road map for Christian living. Love is the binding element for unity in Christ. I have now chosen to love more because you never know the demons people are fighting. Or maybe you *do*—and one act of love might change their direction. Either way, God allowed me to suffer through the situation so I could learn that I am not God and I am not allowed to judge or convict someone of their sins. Only He can do that.

As for me, the pain of my decision will never leave, but the lesson has been learned. I am a better person because of it.

I love you, Susi.

REFLECTIVE QUESTIONS

Is there someone in your life you have turned your back on? Write about that situation.

_____

_____

_____

_____

_____

What can you do to change the direction of that relationship?

_____

_____

_____

_____

_____

What virtues do you need to work on so you might follow Paul's "rules" for a Christian life?

_____

_____

_____

_____

_____

Chapter 9

TRANSFORMATION

1 JOHN 4:7-11

"Dear friends, let us love one another, for love comes from God. Everyone who loves has been born of God and knows God. Whoever does not love does not know God, because God is love. This is how God showed His love among us: He sent His one and only Son into the world that we may live through Him. This is love: not that we loved God, but that He loved us and sent His Son as an atoning sacrifice for our sins. Dear friends, since God so loved us, we ought to love one another."

John was an apostle of Christ. To earn the title "apostle" a person needed to have been with Jesus from His baptism to His ascension. He saw Him, talked with Him, ate with Him, laughed with Him, and watched as He was crucified on the cross. From the very beginning, John was a disciple and friend of Jesus.

The letter of First John was written to remove any doubt and build assurance by clarifying who Christ was. He was fully God and fully man. *Immanuel.* Which means *God with us.* In John's first letter, God isn't only presented as love; he is also shown as light and life. John explains how we, his "dear children" (1 John 3:7), should not be led astray. To be right is righteous; to sin is to turn to Satan and away from the love of God, who sent His Son as our sacrifice for sin to defeat Satan's work in our lives. There could be no greater act of love from God than sending His child to die for our sins so we may have eternal life. We are saved by God's grace through faith in Jesus Christ. This is true love eternal.

As humans with free will, we will no doubt be led astray at some point. The question is: how far astray will we get? I distinctly remember asking Jesus into my heart. This came at a time in my life when I fully regretted the majority of decisions I had made from my mid-teens until I was about 20. There was no way to be forgiven for the sins I had committed. At the time I asked God to come into my life I had lived thirty-four years without knowing God. I started to attend church at the invitation of our Realtor, Marcie Anderson Myers, when we first moved to Canton. Initially, going to church was more to appease her than it was something to take seriously. I didn't even know what purpose it would serve other than making Marcie happy. I would go once to get it over with and then I would get my Sundays back to what I wanted.

I jokingly told Jeanine that the church would fall down around me when I walked in. I told her to stay outside until I went in to make sure that no earthquake destroyed the building. Of course, that was quite the exaggeration, but I really felt that this was simply going through some motions to make a couple of people happy so I could get them off my back. The church would never accept me, I was sure, even though they had no idea of my past transgressions.

We walked in: no earthquake. Step one complete. Step two was not making eye contact with anyone so they wouldn't be obligated to speak to me or I to them. I just wanted to find a seat in the back of the sanctuary—or even in the parking lot if I could get away with it.

Even trying to hide, people came up and welcomed us to the church. I have to admit it was unsettling at first because I really didn't want to know these people. The more people who introduced themselves, the more people I would see in public later who asked me why I hadn't come back to church. I certainly didn't want that kind of pressure! Even though I was still twelve years from my diagnosis, I look back now on the amount of anxiety I had in certain situations. Sure, everyone gets nervous in new surroundings, but this was different. I couldn't breathe at times. I felt strangled and closed in. Kind of like when you try to hold your breath underwater for as long as you can and, when you surface, you feel the exhilaration of air in your lungs again. I was underwater sitting in church and, when I left, the air rushed back into my lungs.

After all that anxiety, something drew me back the next week. Maybe I heard something that Pastor Barr said the first time and I wanted to go back and get more information. Maybe I knew that Jeanine loved being back in church, and the truth was I wanted to go for her. Maybe I still felt obligated to Marcie. I honestly don't know what happened that brought me back, but I sure know now. The Holy Spirit was working in my life to draw me closer to God. Of course, at that time, I didn't know the difference between God, Jesus, and the Holy Spirit. To be honest, I barely knew that Jesus was the Son of God. I thought he was just a character in some two thousand-page book. I thought Jesus wrote the whole book! I was really confused why everything Jesus said was in red in the Bible! Regardless, there I was for a second week in a row. I kept thinking that someone from my past life would come into the church and call me out. I didn't need that kind of anxiety on top of what I was already feeling. But it never happened.

So many questions popped into my head. If I go to church, can I still have a beer? Priorities, right? I used vulgar words more than I would like to admit. Do I have to stop saying them? Do I need to wear a suit? I don't even own a suit. What is this plate being passed around with little pieces of stale bread and grape juice? A snack during the service? How does everyone know the words to these songs without looking at the music book? (Yes, I really called it "a music book" before I knew it was called a hymnal.) So many rules. I told myself: I guess at some point I'll need to ask and answer all of these questions if I'm going to continue going.

What I learned from my extremely trying first few church visits was that, despite everything I had done, God loves me. I don't question it now, but I sure questioned it then. As John stated, God *is* love. From my first church visit to dealing with my disorder on a daily basis, God has proven His love for me over and over again. When I am battling to just get up each morning, God is there as my eternal alarm clock. I may hit snooze a few times, but God will wait. If he can forgive a sinner like me—and He had such love for me that He sent Jesus to die on behalf of my sins—well . . . it makes my issues seem trivial when I am in the right frame of mind.

My routine each morning is to pray and read devotionals. It used to be grabbing my phone and seeing what all my friends had to say on social media. I found that my relationship with God is much more meaningful than any political argument on social media. I ask the Holy Spirit to come into my heart and reflect through me His grace and glory so people will see I am a child of God. That kind of peace cannot be replaced by the instant gratification of a peach cobbler recipe or a friend's opinion on how to solve the problems of the world. God's love is eternal. Peach cobbler is temporary.

I struggle sometimes to find the right words to pray, but God knows what I need. Yesterday I was so manic I couldn't string two words together. Yet I prayed the best I could to God and He listened to my rambling needs. I have come to the realization that my prayers don't have to be so formal. I don't have to speak eloquently for God to listen. That's good because when I am manic or depressed, my prayers sometimes do not make sense. They are all over the board. But while I need to glorify God in all I do, including prayer, I think God cuts me some slack when I don't have just the right words. He always knows what I need: up to and including a peaceful, rational mind.

Sometimes it takes patience for God to answer, but He will. Do you know why? Because He loves us and always takes care of His children. From thinking the church will crumble around me to knowing that God loves me no matter what—that is quite the transformation.

I didn't see it coming, but God knew exactly what He was doing. Even with a sinner like me.

Reflective Questions

Have you come to a point in which you trust God? When did that begin?

_____

_____

_____

_____

_____

How does God show His love in your life? Write about some of his specific acts of kindness to you.

_____

_____

_____

_____

_____

What are some routines you can change on a daily basis to glorify God more?

_____

_____

_____

_____

_____

Chapter 10

LEARNING TO LOVE

Luke 6:35, 36
"But love your enemies, do good to them,
and lend to them without expecting to get
anything back. Then your reward will be great, and
you will be children of the Most High because
He is kind to the ungrateful and wicked. Be merciful,
just as your Father is merciful."

Jesus is teaching the people how to lead a life that glorifies God. He is giving instructions on how to have eternal life through Him. The book of Luke lays out the life of Christ from His birth to His ascension. It is sometimes used at Christmas during Christmas programs or in storytelling to children. Luke is the only Gentile Christian author in the New Testament, and he tells a very comprehensive account of Jesus' life.

This is the first of Luke's two books of the Bible, along with Acts. Luke, along with Paul, became extremely vocal in proclaiming the Good News despite persecution. Luke also became Paul's personal physician and one of his closest friends all the way up to Paul being tried, convicted, and sentenced to death in Rome around A.D. 67. In 2 Timothy 4:9-11, Paul appeals to Timothy to *"do your best to come to me quickly"* (verse 9) because Demas, Crescens, and Titus all had deserted him (v. 10), and, Paul writes to Timothy, *"Only Luke is with me"* (v. 11). I truly believe he was present for Paul's execution.

Love your enemies. This statement seems like an oxymoron to me. If you show people love, typically they are close to you. I've not had a lot of enemies, but the last thing I think of with the few I've had is love, and I certainly don't want them close to me. But Jesus tells us differently. Jesus doesn't tell us to love our enemies in the way that you love a family member or close friend. Or does He? Jesus tells us to *show mercy* on them. To pray for them. To seriously think of ways for them not to be your enemy. Could he be saying that anyone who doesn't know Him and the way to eternal life is an "enemy"? It seems like a stretch, but hear me out. Jesus loves us all—Jew and Gentile, believers and nonbelievers—despite the sins we've committed. Jesus ate dinner with tax collectors and sinners (Luke 5:29-31). When the Pharisees and teachers of the law saw this, they asked him, "Why do you eat and drink with tax collectors and sinners?" (5:30) Jesus answered: "It is not the healthy that need a doctor, but the sick. I have not come to call the righteous but sinners to repentance" (5:31).

As I stated, I really have no enemies (that I know of). I try to be respectful and kind to everyone. I will engage in discussion if someone is disrespectful to me, but no matter the outcome, I don't "hate" them or consider them my enemy. It can be difficult to stay rational if I feel someone has wronged me or my family. I can get irritated rather quickly and hold a grudge. I call this "protection mode," but you know what? Jesus will have none of it. In Mark 12:30, 31, Jesus says: *"Love the Lord your God with all of your heart and with all of your soul and with all of your mind and with all of your strength. The second is this: love your neighbor as yourself. There is no commandment greater than these."* Whoa! No greater commandment than these? I told you that Jesus will not have any of my "protection mode" nonsense. Of all the commands that Jesus gives us, loving God and loving your neighbor is the greatest of all? I need an attitude check. I get the loving God part. That should be the greatest command. But I never would have thought that loving my neighbor, Rod, would even enter Jesus' mind. (Just kidding, Rod!)

In my life, this is a roller coaster that never ends. I have to come to grips with the grace and mercy God has shown me. During some cycles, I have angry moments. I'm not really angry at anyone. Just . . . *angry*. I can't explain it or predict when it will happen. I just know that the last thing on my mind is forgiving people I feel have wronged me.

I once had a situation in which I trusted someone to pay me back money I fronted them for the cost of a visitation and funeral until the life insurance money came. The total amount was $7,500, and my sister Lori paid half. When the insurance check was issued, the person who received it took off with the money. Never to be heard from again. Angry doesn't even come close to describing how I felt. Someone I trusted to do the right thing took advantage of the situation and kept all the money for themselves. *And* . . . this person is family. This is the one time in my life I came closest to hating someone. As a Christian, I know to turn the other cheek when someone hits me. This punch happened to be straight on my nose, so there wasn't a cheek to turn! I don't think I have taken as many Xanax as I took for the six months after this happened! There was no way I would ever forgive this person.

But I knew this was wrong, so I cried out to God to please show me the way to get past it. As time went by, the pain of betrayal, by the grace of God, became less and less. I would be lying if I said that during my angry times, when I think about it, I don't get just as mad as the first day it happened. This is the irrational side of the disorder coming out. But it was the grace and love of God that got me through that very angry period—and continues to do so. He has softened my heart to the situation, and I have realized that I need to be the same model to everyone that I encounter. While I will never forget the hurt that this family member caused, I have forgiven them. I even pray for them daily. If this person showed up on my doorstep today, I would have a lot of questions for them, but I would let them in.

Going through life holding onto a situation that has caused me to be bitter and angry is not what God wants me to do. I pray each day for the Holy Spirit to work through me, and part of that work is showing love and grace to others.

The mercy and love Jesus showed to those who were considered evil by the people, as those who didn't have faith, set the example for the rest of us to become disciples of Christ and spread the Good News. And that's to everyone, not just people within our congregation. We have to step out of our comfort zone and spread the Word so all people have the opportunity to be saved by grace through faith.

While nonbelievers are not enemies in the sense we typically think of, they are on a losing battlefield when compared with all of us who believe. They are on a path to spend eternity in Hell if they fail to repent. As we fight the battle for eternal salvation, we should give nonbelievers the opportunity to join us on our side of the battle. We should issue the command to not engage our "enemies" in battle, but to show the same mercy that God has shown us for the cause of bringing eternal life to all people.

In no way do I want this to sound like Christians are better than nonbelievers. That type of arrogance is just as sinful as disobeying God's commands for us. I truly believe it is our call to give the facts of salvation and then respect the decisions of those who hear those facts whether we agree with how they respond or not. To continue to love them no matter their opinions. Others may view my opinion of the definition of an enemy as radical or just flat wrong. I truly respect that. My interpretation falls strictly on me. But regardless of your stance, it is our job as Christians to speak the truth of the glory of God and the path to eternal life through Christ Jesus to all people, including those who may not have the same views and mission in life we do.

They are not your enemies. They are children of God just waiting to hear the Good News. Give it to them.

REFLECTIVE QUESTIONS

Is there a person—or certain people, from a certain situation—who you need to forgive?

_____

_____

_____

_____

_____

How will you ask God to help you forgive?

_____

_____

_____

_____

_____

How do you handle situations when someone doesn't agree with you? How can you handle them better?

_____

_____

_____

_____

_____

Chapter 11

THE HIDDEN ENEMY

With this chapter I'm going to stray from the "love" theme of this section. As I thought through the title for this chapter, I tried to find words to reflect my feelings and prayed for direction. Over the last few days, God spoke to me about the content and tenor of the words. It has been a while since the presence of God was this strong. He spoke to me about continuing my journey. I had a constant feeling that it is time to start again. So here I am. Sitting at my new computer. Writing for the first time in a very long time. He is with me, and I am His vessel.

The last time I opened this book was February 18, 2020. That day, my passion for putting thoughts into words stopped. I had no desire to think, write, or share feelings. The journey came to an end. I thought about trashing the whole thing. I've heard of writer's block before, but this seemed different. I wasn't struggling to find the words; I didn't *want* to write the words. All thought processes pertaining to this book stopped. I was done. A book that I spent so many hours on with so many tears had come to completion even though I didn't feel it was complete. The book would never be published. All of the work for nothing. I was defeated.

Today, December 26, 2020, the burning desire to share my journey is flaring up inside me again. God is back in control. God has told me that it's time. The experiences of the last ten months are worthy of His voice speaking through me again. During those months I thought about the book often and the sudden halt to God's voice, the voice that had driven me to share my most intimate thoughts and feelings.

I even tried to force it at times. Opening the manuscript to try to continue. Nothing. Not one thought. Not one voice leading me. I closed the document even more confused than before.

Now I understand. God had a plan, and I was trying to force my personal agenda. I reflect back and feel ashamed that I put my desires over His. People would ask me about the progress of the book and I would merely smile and tell them it was coming along. I didn't have the courage to say that the passion had ended. I felt embarrassed that I had hyped the book and it might never come to fruition.

But today, this day, God has put me back on track. To those who asked me about the progress and I skirted the issue, I'm sorry. I should have been honest with you. But I had no idea what to say. I continued to avoid the subject hoping that the darkness of the situation would soon give way to God's ever-present light, a light I had obviously shielded my eyes from. And just like Paul, the scales have been lifted from my eyes, and I continue my journey to follow God's path and the bright light He provides for me.

Our world has been turned upside down by a pandemic. As of this date, December 26, 2020, more than 80 million cases of COVID-19 worldwide, and 1.75 million deaths, have resulted—with no end in sight, even with a newly developed vaccine. The pandemic has tested the resolve of all of God's people. People have not been able to live a normal life because of the fear that grips the world on a daily basis. Businesses shuttered, millions of people have lost their jobs, families not able to spend time together, and there are the seemingly never-ending stories of people sharing the pain of adjusting their lives because they lost someone close to them. The world was stressful enough before the emergence of the pandemic affected everyone on the planet. Many studies indicate the number of people who experienced mental health issues during the pandemic increased dramatically. In some areas of the world suicide rates increased by double-digit percentages.

I now know that God halted the progress of this book so that, ten months later, I could begin to write again and share my experiences living daily with Bipolar Disorder along with the addition of the stress and worry of an uncontrollable pandemic.

For the first seven weeks of the pandemic shutdown in Illinois, I worked from home. The uncertainty of the virus and my underlying health issues had me concerned enough to not go out in public. Those who know me know that this almost killed me. I'm a worker and a fixer. I need to have those daily challenges to keep me going and to keep my mind occupied. While I had my wife by my side and I truly enjoyed her company, those were the longest seven weeks of my life. I soon found out that a "work from home" job wasn't for me, and I threw all caution to the wind and physically went back to the office. I needed to be there for my team but, mostly, for me.

As I have described several times in this book, even getting out of bed each day can be a challenge. To add the stress and worry of a pandemic just escalates my daily struggles. Even more so, lifelong friends have turned against each other because of differing domestic and world views. Social media has turned into a bitter, hateful arena that has turned everyone into a keyboard warrior for advancing their agenda. The majority of the people who comment would not have the courage to say the things they say face to face.

I had one friend who cleared out his "friends" list of everyone he knew didn't have the same political ideology he did. I had another who deleted all of his social media accounts to stop all of the madness. This is the world we have turned into, and I pray daily for my Savior to come back.

When I wake up, I thank God for another day. Then I pick up my phone and expose myself to hate and death. I should know better. The first thing I should do is turn my eyes toward Jesus. However, I'm human, and I let the news and views of the day engulf me. I have found myself adding Xanax to my daily medicine, which was previously used only for instant-onset symptoms, instead of turning away and focusing on God. In Jeremiah 25:32 the prophet wrote, *"This is what the Lord Almighty says: Look! Disaster is spreading from nation to nation; a mighty storm is rising from the ends of the earth."* I find myself getting caught up in the disaster that is taking place all around me. We are self-destructing from the inside out because we choose to follow the events of the day and not the ultimate goal of choosing Christ over all else. I am not guiltless in all of this. I continually ask for God's forgiveness while I am in this broken world.

Anxiety is enhanced by outside stimuli. It's bad enough that I get anxious about the demons I may fight in a day. The outside noise ramps up and adds more to my plate of worry: the seemingly never-ending news about a pandemic that is killing millions; the worry of when, not if, it will affect my loved ones; the fear that I may have a loved one who gets so sick from this virus that they might be hospitalized and I will not be allowed to be with them. Story after story of people dying alone while their family waits helplessly for news.

As I write this, I am becoming more amped up with the mere thought of any of these things happening. I have my Bible sitting next to me; I'm scanning for anything that will give me comfort. What I need to realize is that the entire Book should give me comfort. God's words in book form. Page after page of comfort, peace, and healing. There is nothing in His Book that he wouldn't say to me face to face. I must trust that this is a friendship that lasts forever no matter what I may say to anger Him. This is the model we should strive to adhere to instead of the model of hate and despair.

He is the friend request who we have all been waiting for, and I should accept His request unconditionally. There is no way to stop the train wreck that has already happened, but if we love God with every ounce of who we are, He can build the perfect track that leads directly to Him. May His will be done in my life and in this sinful world.

Reflective Questions

List three strong feelings you experienced during the trials of 2020-2021.

_____

_____

_____

_____

_____

How could you have handled those feelings better? How might you have turned to God in a more spiritual way?

_____

_____

_____

_____

_____

How can you focus more on God instead of social media or the news?

_____

_____

_____

_____

_____

Chapter 12

HOW GOD PROVIDES: A WAY TO HELP

GALATIANS 6:2
*"Carry each other's burdens, and in this way
you will fulfill the law of Christ."*

You know someone who has a mental illness or you, yourself, suffer from a mental illness. It's inevitable (unless you live an extremely sheltered life with no human contact, and that is not likely). They are all around you—and you may not even know them. Many people put on a "brave" face—I'm not a fan of that saying—and take on the world. That struggling person around you may be the guy who changes your oil, or the lady who waits on you at the grocery store, or even your family doctor. Mental illness is not choosy. It can affect anyone at any time. All races, ages, sex, social status, and professions. Some people are highly functioning and some people need to be treated in a mental health facility. I am one of the blessed ones who can continue to work.

I have been in the credit union industry for the better part of thirty-three years. The last seventeen years have been at an executive level. There is a lot of pressure that goes with the responsibility of millions of dollars of other people's money. But I hit that job head-on each day. There are days when I'm just not feeling I can do my job or my coworkers any justice, but I am blessed with a very understanding boss and staff who know just the right ways to support me. For the most part, I feel I rock my position and try to never use my disorder as a crutch. If the demons are too loud, I stay home. Most people don't know I have a daily battle beyond my career. I would prefer to keep it that way, but God wants me to tell my story. So here I am.

Taking all this into account, I have thought, for a long time, about the people I encounter who suffer from demons. Sitting in a conference room of people (back when we could still pack a conference room) and wondering how many people struggle in silence. Attending church on Sunday knowing that there are others similar to me with similar struggles. What would it take for them to break their silence? An understanding friend or family member? A complete mental break that leaves them with no choice but to disclose their battle? A group of people who listened and understood what they were going through?

In early 2020, God placed an opportunity directly in front of me and several people in our church. My good friend, Kari Brown, sent me some information about an opportunity to become a Certified First Responder Mental Health Coach. The course is offered through Light University, which is backed by the American Association of Christian Counselors (AACC). It is a 40-hour biblically based certification led by some of the best mental health professionals in the world. As I read through the syllabus, I knew immediately that this was a course I needed; I signed up on the spot.

I want to clarify: we are not professional counselors. Counselors go through years of training to be able to diagnose and treat all forms of mental illness. The purpose of our ministry as coaches is to assess a situation, take a biblical approach to jointly discuss, hopefully assist the person through their struggles, and refer them to professionals if necessary.

At the same time, Pastor Matt learned about the opportunity and made it available to our church members with the cost being picked up by the church. It is an opportunity to offer mental health coaching to people who have been silent about what they suffer with. A light to shine on all people who live in darkness, not just Christians. An outreach that has been absent and is much needed. This was the beginning of something beautiful and, more importantly, God-led.

Pastor Matt and I met to discuss the impact that this type of training could have, not only in our church but also in our community. Pastor Matt has been so influential in my continued discussions of the issues of mental health in the Christian community. I have had many meetings with him just to bounce ideas off him regarding how we can bring light to the shadows and expose the silent crisis. All of this was before the opportunity that AACC afforded us.

Do you see the picture God has painted? God put Pastor Matt in my life as a sounding board for my passion for bringing awareness regarding mental health issues to the Christian community. I distinctly remember Pastor Matt saying in one of the early discussions that we need a safe place for people to talk openly about their struggles. God then presented the opportunity to us in the form of mental health coaching. This is a new ministry that is so needed and has not been available anywhere in our area. All I could think about is how awesome our God is and how faithful He is to us if we are just patient. We can deliver a much-needed rope of life to people in need.

The Evangelical Free Church of Canton's Mental Health Ministry is now underway. We had our first planning session in early 2021 with thirteen loving, committed people in attendance and many more who couldn't attend. We talked about how the ministry can impact so many people within our community. I had the honor of leading the planning session knowing that every person in attendance had a servant's heart and was put in their chair by God Himself. I sat in a room of people who want to help break the stigma and silence of mental health.

Each person had his or her own story of why they wanted to be part of this groundbreaking opportunity. Some stories were for personal reasons due to mental health affecting them in different ways. Other stories were about a selfless act of love for other people. No matter the reason, God put us together in that room to advance His ministry. Throughout the earlier times when Pastor Matt and I were talking about the stigma of mental health, God was planning this moment to put His support group together.

I was scheduled to speak to our church in May 2020, but the talk was canceled due to Covid. Instead, I put together a short video that was shown during an online church service that outlined this book and some about my journey. I have had many people within our congregation approach me once my story was told. People who, from the outside, look polished and successful. On the inside, however, they are broken, scared, and confused. One person even shared with me that they have had suicidal thoughts and asked why God didn't intervene. These types of discussions are what is missing in the Christian community. It's time to end that stigma.

The ministry training outlines the various types of coaching opportunities we may encounter. Bipolar Disorder, depression, Post-Traumatic Stress Disorder, various types of addiction, grief, suicidal thoughts, anxiety, and situational mental health. The training through Light University is extensive and difficult, but our group members have lovingly given their time to become certified coaches. Some have gone on to get separate, specialized certifications such as dealing with grief, addiction, and anxiety care.

I'm excited to see what God has in store for the ministry. My heart is full that He chose me to be part of the solution for such a silent topic. If you would like more information about the mental health first responder coaching curriculum, please visit www.lightuniversity.com or the American Association of Christian Counselors at: www.aacc.net.

REFLECTIVE QUESTIONS

Do you see the need for mental health coaching in your congregation? If yes, write about the needs you see.

_____

_____

_____

_____

_____

How can you work with your church leadership to bring mental health coaching to your church?

_____

_____

_____

_____

_____

What is your motivation for wanting to help others who struggle with mental health issues?

_____

_____

_____

_____

_____

Chapter 13

'THE GREATEST OF THESE'

1 CORINTHIANS 13:13
*"And now these three remain: faith, hope,
and love. But the greatest of these is love."*

Love sounds so simple. I was reading through the reference section of my Bible and saw there are at least eighty-one Scriptures or passages of Scripture that reference love. I'm sure there are more than that, but the editor of the *Life Application Study Bible* probably said something like, "Okay. That should be enough to get you started." Love your neighbor, love your God, love your husband, love your wife, love is patient, love is kind, and the list goes on. When I think of love, I think of someone giving of themselves, and you to them, unconditionally, with the whole heart. That's it. There is nothing else.

Many people see and refer to love as strictly an emotion. I love steak, I love Smarties, I love to fish, and I love the Alabama Crimson Tide. But the thing is, none of those things can love me back. This type of love truly is emotion-based. Maybe a better way of putting it is that I *enjoy* steak, I *enjoy* Smarties, and I *enjoy* fishing. (I still love the Crimson Tide, and I would like to think they love me back.)

I look back on my life and realize I have one regret: I started smoking at age 15, and I still smoke to this day. You could say that I love—no, *enjoy*—smoking. Such a filthy habit that has a stronghold on my life. While I have cut down my daily smoking considerably, I just can't find a way to break the chain. You would think that watching my father die from emphysema would be motivation enough. Evidently, it isn't. I look at all of the life events that I'm sure I will eventually miss. Mainly, my grandchildren graduating from school, watching them get married, having children of their own. I would love that, but I think the damage is done even if I would quit today. This is the one area of my life in which, truthfully, I haven't loved myself enough to stop something, and that something will eventually kill me.

It weighs on me, and I pray about it daily. The never-ending love of God doesn't seem to be enough in this case. I'm not blaming Him; this is my free will choice to continue. I wish I had the strength and love for myself to stop. I have to do it for me over anyone else. I know it hurts my family to watch me continue to put nails in my coffin one cigarette at a time. They continue to love me despite all that. I have defeated so many daily demons. But I ask for your prayers of love and strength as I battle this demon that seemingly won't go away.

The ultimate purpose of this book is to explain the correlation of my journey with Bipolar Disorder and my walk with God and to give Him all the glory for my life, no matter how imperfect it is. His love for me is the foundation of my daily existence. The love of God transcends any other love we can fathom. Our human minds can't grasp the full depth. 1 Chronicles 16:34 says, *"Give thanks to the Lord, for He is good. His love endures forever."* Not just today, not just tomorrow, not even in our earthly life. Forever. From Genesis to Revelation and forever in His heavenly kingdom, I have the love of God.

The mere thought of this overwhelms me. If you are ready to surrender and have never asked Christ into your heart, now is the time. It's simple: "Lord Jesus, I know that I'm a sinner and I need your forgiveness and love. I want to turn away from my sins and ask you into my heart. I want to be your child so that I may have eternal life. I trust and love you, Lord. Your will be done in my life."

This is your prayer of salvation. My hope is that you will ask and that you will be blessed with life for all eternity with Him.

There is no way to count the number of times in my life I have turned against God and sinned. But His love endures. His love endures during my anger. His love endures during my suicidal thoughts. His love endures during my panic attacks. His love endures during my manic episodes. His love endures during my sinful actions. I am certainly not worthy. I'm not worthy of this life He has entrusted me with. I have failed Him along the way. But there are 66 books and 1,189 chapters in the Bible that remind me of His unwavering love and faithfulness as His child. Just read Lamentations 3:22, 23 if you need confirmation: *"Because of the Lord's great love, we are not consumed. For His compassions never fail. They renew every morning; great is your faithfulness."* His compassions renew . . . every . . . morning. Trust me: I need His compassions to renew every morning. To wipe away the slate from the previous day and allow me to start anew.

I'm sure you have noticed, probably ad nauseam, that I continually repeat that He will never leave you, that you should cry out to Him, that He will never forsake you, and He loves you. This is by design. You may have said: "Okay, okay, I get it." But you need to hear it. I need to hear it. We all need to know the seriousness of the love God has for us. He is your Father and you are His child. Parents don't abandon their children and God will never abandon you.

I love you. I may not even know you, but I love you nevertheless. It is what I am called to do. God calls me to do that. Jesus calls me to do that. The apostle Paul calls me to do that. I wear that command like a badge of honor. It is my pleasure to love you. I pray for you daily. You are worthy of my love. You are beautiful because God created you. You are my brother or sister, maybe not by blood, but because we are both children of God.

Love transcends all things. If we can't love or pray for one another, we have no hope. The hope that we will one day stand face to face with God the Father no matter our impurities or the mental ailments that haunted us for our entire earthly life. Eternity awaits us. Our minds, which failed us in this world, will be healed. Our thoughts of self-harm, self-worth, and self-image will not even be a memory. We will be born again, and we will be perfect. Just as the perfect Lamb was sent to this world so we may have eternal life. That is the love God shows us. *That* is the compassion that has followed us during our time on earth. Some days we see it and some days it seems so far away. But it's there.

If you get nothing else from this book, know that you are not alone. Your thoughts, at times, are raw and confusing—but they are valid. No one has the right to downplay what you are feeling. You have the right to feel what you are feeling. God understands your pain and wants so badly for you to cry out to Him. He is your comfort, your unconditional love, your soft place to land. He has put people in your life who can help you out of the seemingly endless trials of pain and despair. Use them. They love you and care about you. You just have to talk to them. Tell them how you are feeling. Ask them for love and understanding.

Relate this to the people you love: No matter what they may do, you will show them unconditional love to get them through it. Now, you also have to do the same thing for yourself. Allow others to show you the same unconditional love you show them. If you are hurting, reach out. Do not take this on yourself. Jesus said that when two or more are gathered in His name, He will be there. Sit and talk with a loved one and know that the strength of God is with you as you talk.

There is nothing you can say that will separate you from God's love. And I'm going to go out on a limb and say it will also not separate you from the ones you love. May Christ reign forever in your life, and may His power overcome the demons you fight. He will be victorious, and you will survive knowing that God's protection and love got you through it. In your darkest times, my hope . . . my *prayer* . . . is for you to remember that God will never leave you. Neither will I. I love you. Never forget that.

About the Author and This Book

Paul was born and raised in Hanna City, Illinois, a small community just west of Peoria. He lives with his family today in Canton, Illinois.

He is Chief Operations Officer of the Illinois Educators Credit Union in Springfield, Illinois. 2021 marked his thirty-third year in the credit union industry, in which he has worked his way from a document runner to his current position. The credit union industry is a passion of Paul's and gives him the opportunity to work daily with people in all stages of life.

After being diagnosed with Bipolar II Disorder in 2012, Paul felt he had a higher calling, one in which he could talk about his disorder. In the back of his mind, he knew that men are "not supposed to talk about" their feelings. He felt by speaking about his feelings he wouldn't be able to be the strength his family needed. Only after he felt God speaking to him about being a vessel for change in the way Christians approach mental illness did he begin to speak more openly about it. God's calling led to this book.

Paul has been married to his wife, Jeanine, for 33 years. He has three children, Shane, Chase, and Allyson, along with seven grandchildren.

Paul feels deeply about breaking the stigma of mental health in the Christian community, and he hopes this book will begin discussions that, until this point, are usually kept in the shadows. The book is available to anyone. While it has a suggested retail price, Paul wants to make sure *A Walk with the Light in the Shadows* gets in the hands of anyone who needs it. If you know someone who can't afford the asking price, have them send what they can. It will be available on the website www.walkwiththelight.com for whatever donation a person can make. Paul will make sure a book gets in that person's hands.

You can contact Paul through his website or at awalkwiththelight@gmail.com if you would like to talk about your struggles or invite him to speak at your church or community event.

With each church visit, a percentage of proceeds from each book sold will be donated to the church. For books purchased online, a percentage of the proceeds will be donated to Faith Bible Camp. For more information about the camp, please visit www.faithbiblecamp.com.

#BipolarChristian

#endthestigma

#awalkwiththelightintheshadows